# TIPPING POINT

D0851383

# TIPPING POINT

Fred Marchant

*[signature: Fred Marchant]*

*Winner of the 1993 Word Works Washington Prize*

The Word Works • Washington, DC

Printed in the U.S.A.
Book design, typography: Joyce Mulcahy, Jude Langsam
Cover art: Nona Hershey, "Profile," 1986, etching

Library of Congress Number: 93-061079

International Standard Book Number: 0-915380-30-7

A number of these poems (or earlier versions of them) have
appeared in the following: *AGNI:* "Boraxo," "Hospital
Food," "Rescue," "Wartime," "Whiskey"; *America:* "Mayan
Figures in Stone"; *Aspect:* "Baptismal Photograph"; *The Boston
Phoenix:* "Magnification"; *The Boston Review:* "Butterfly Chair";
*Bristlecone:* "Demby in the River"; *Connecticut Poetry Review:*
"State Lines," "Vietnam Era"; *Ellipsis:* "Directions Down";
*Gettysburg Review:* "Bristlecone"; *Harvard Review:* "Song of the
Stomach," "Tipping Point," "The Afterlife on Squaw Peak";
*Poetry Northwest:* "Minotaur"; *Ploughshares:* "Walden,"
"Lazarus," "Stillness in South Carolina"; *Southern Humanities
Review:* "Herons"; *Tampa Review:* "C.O."; *Worcester Review:*
"Certain Obliquities, and Then Loss"; *Yankee:* "Lines After
Buson."

My thanks to the MacDowell Colony, the Ucross Foundation,
and Yaddo for residencies during which this book was
completed. I would also like to thank the Suffolk University
College of Liberal Arts and Sciences for ongoing support. I
am deeply grateful to those friends and teachers whose
careful readings helped bring this book into being. Finally,
my gratitude to my editor, Barbara Goldberg, is woven
throughout this work.

For Stefi

# CONTENTS

IV

V

## DIRECTIONS DOWN

*First, you will have to cross*
*a talus slope, stretches of*
*sphagnum and low growth fern,*
*a purple cluster of lupine.*

*Then down through the dwarfed*
*evergreens, moss-shrouded,*
*miraculous to the touch,*
*the bark smooth as new flesh.*

*Hold onto whatever offers itself.*
*Be thankful for the roots rising*
*like knuckles and fists, and*
*for the deadfall which will stop*

*you should you trip. You might*
*feel the impulse to linger awhile,*
*maybe to listen to the wood thrush,*
*but the light will be dimming,*

*and there will be the knife-*
*edge, the sheer drop, the stones*
*unwilling to stand still and*
*pass you on gently to the next.*

*When you smell our cooking fires*
*and hear our prayers mingling,*
*we will know you are near.*
*We may be feeling ashamed*

*of the flaws you will find in us,*
*of the mistakes we have made,*
*of the crude place we have built*
*for you to live among us.*

*But we are part of who you are,*
*and we have been waiting a long time.*
*We are glad now to see you.*
*Oh, angel, landed, stay.*

I

## BAPTISMAL PHOTOGRAPH

A January afternoon
in black and white,
the shadow of a tree limb
crosses our bodies—

me and my grim Irish grandfather.
I am freezing and furious
and swaddled in lace.
He seems preoccupied with

age, his weak arms and heart,
how bitter the cold is.
A scarf protects his ears.
His gabardine coat is

buttoned to the throat.
The sun is in his eyes,
and he will not smile.
He'd rather die than drop me.

## WHISKEY

It was his mother he saw
at the bottom of the bottle,
saw her surrounded by dried
bouquets, adrift on a deep
brown sea where outcrops
of love looked just like
the baskets the Lutherans
delivered to the immigrant
widow and her boy, who now
saw himself standing at the door
bringing the pilgrim and parson
into the warm kitchen to unpack
the coffee rings dusted with
snowy sugar, and the Svenska talk
swelling through the tenement:
"Gut Yul" and "Nay, tak" and
in passing, someone noting how
the sky was lowering, old-country
cold, and that the first-born
could with his milk, "Sure!"
have his first taste.

## THE FOOT OF THE MOUNTAIN

Before I learned to speak
I knew what my father's hand
sounded like when it struck
my mother on the face.

I could tell from afar
and from under the pillow
the difference between
an open palm and the fist.

Slap was precise, pointed,
and lightning clear.
Afterward, the air was almost
sweet with particles of relief.

Punch—strange, goofy
word—was a furtive,
inward-looking sound,
as if it hoped it had not been heard.

Curses too sounded like slap
and punch. "Bastard"
clattered through the air.
"Sonofabitch," however,

sucked the breath out.
I had no idea of meaning,
but rather, the tones I heard
were the pure being of these.

Now my father can hardly speak.
His lungs move only enough air
across his cords to whisper,
or whistle involuntarily.

Maybe he wants to say,
"Forgive me," but always
there has been nothing
but a steep granite silence

between us, and it is now
all the more brilliant
and uninviting in the clear
blue light at the top.

## MAGNIFICATION

Roseate spoonbills—shy, retreating
into the mangrove. The guidebook
says the species has been battered
and does not trust us. I stand at the rail
overlooking the pan-flat, tidal swamp,
adjusting the field glasses, my eyes
training on the mostly still, nearly
camouflaged smudges of pink.

In my tightened breathing, in the light
through the vines in the distant hollow
I see a moment of my own waking—
me a first-grader on a long oak bench,
my mother and I waiting for a train,
the sunlight marching through wired,
cathedral windows, and dust floating,
upheld in the beams, the pigeons cooing.

My mother's cheek bruised blue-green.
A welt high on her nose where her
glasses pressed. This was flight,
her intended escape down the Eastern
seaboard. I was deep in my bright
comic, one of the *Tales of the Unknown,*
and nibbling from my stash a crumbly,
cheese-flavored, peanut-butter cracker.

Suddenly a whistle bored in, the marble
floor shuddered, and the *Minuteman*'s bell
sounded frantic, mad. Overhead, a voice
announced, magnified, and distorted
the names of what lay before us.
Pigeons leapt into the lime-streaked vault.
We gathered together what we had
and took our two places in the line.

## BUTTERFLY CHAIR

I can see it again tonight in rough outline
        where the clear-cuts
        rise and slant up the valley:

the middle room of the flat where I grew up,
        a corner space for the television
        where I watched

the quarrels spill like hot oil flowing from
        kitchen to parlor,
        my father holding my mother

by the forearm to keep her steady while
        he hit her, the two of them
        silvered, and me slung

in the butterfly chair, the rounded canvas
        bottom so deep, my feet
        didn't reach the floor.

Transfixed, a moth awash in the light
        of what it wants so much,
        I would stare through them

into the window of the tube, and its brightness,
        holding onto a glassy wish
        that I would die.

## BORAXO

He would flick his middle finger at the tin,
    and sprinkle out a mound
        of stark, alkaline powder.

Cupping it in his palm, he would begin
    an almost punitive scrub:
        knuckles, wrists, elbows;

rinse, scan for the hidden grease,
    and start again, the soap
        floating an oily, fish-gray skim.

At the table, beaming like a grandee,
    he would rub his palms
        together to hear the hiss

of his own clean dry flesh, and as he
    counted up the blessings:
        house, son, wife,

he would hold his hands out for us to see,
    declaring, "Now *this*,
        this is the life."

## BACKRUB

Watching *The Untouchables,*
      me sitting in front of him
            on an old vinyl hassock,

my shirt off, my back
      football sore, his hands
            kneading around the blades.

I half attend to his words
      about knots, cramps, breathing.

The show's brass din theme
      and gunbursts from *Murder*
            *Incorporated* just barely allow me

to hear a hope in his tone
      that he's done nothing to me
            his strong, thick hands can't fix.

# VIETNAM ERA

In 1959 you were thirteen and rose
         earlier than you ever
imagined, knowing birds had nothing
         on *you*, leaving
on an empty stomach to deliver the news,
         ignoring your mother's
sleepy warnings, beating your lathered
         father out the door,
to hop now on the company bike
         and ride to the station
where your *Globes* and *Heralds* waited
         to be folded and stuffed
into the wire basket, the canvas bag.
         Let everyone else go
fishing: you patrolled an uncharted
         city, a zone dawning
in headlines and traffic. You were
         losing baby fat and
saving money for school. The papers
         you heaved you imagined
grenades, and that the porches they
         landed on burst into flame,
sending the little girls out flying
         straight into your arms,
arms already smeared with the ink
         from the world's bloody
deeds, your own war only seven years away.

## SONG OF THE STOMACH

I do not mean the organ.

I mean the flab, the spare tire, the ring
of flesh I carry with me, and do not love.

I will try to love you.

When I pinch the side and shake you slightly,
I will think of the depths of history
that produced you.

I once mocked myself saying it was an Irish
potato gene that did this to me. Even then
I could hear the several favorable presences
that have always been near, cautioning me
not to be so clever, so flip, to think of
the rheumy, hungry child, and the act of will
that commanded the genes to plan and store up
what little they would have on this earth.

When I pinch the other side, I will remember
my mother, and try to imagine how she must
have hated her corsets. I will remember how
frightening these were, bony medical wraps
with the dangling Eros of straps. I will remember
her saying she needed a new one *to hold her in,*
and my worry that she was being literal,
and my amazement at my father for not
having the money to keep her from spilling out.

I will rub the hair toward the center,
the way it wants to go, and I will not
deny the strange pleasure of holding myself,
of fingering the depth from the brim
to the swirl of the navel.

I will remember the word *Butterball*,
my detested schoolyard name.
I will remember dreading Thanksgiving,
and the ads for basted, dripping rounds of turkey.
I couldn't understand how even I in fat
could be thought to look like that.

*To look like that.*
I will try to remember the origin of my shames.
The quick instinct to cover, to stay underwater,
to slip unnoticed to the sexual sidelines.
I will hate every thought of Darwin.

I will remember too the miraculous onset:
not only hair below to surprise me, but the sleek
suddenness with which the child's body shed
what everyone said was baby fat. My amazement
at the way I was welcomed into the communion
of ordinary bodies. How there were girls
who didn't even know me when I was fat,
who couldn't believe me when I said I was,
or had been, and who were wide-eyed with sweetness
they had no idea they possessed.

With both hands I will hold this portion of myself
before the bright morning of the world.
I will declare it my *felix culpa*,
my fall into the fallen,
my unruly badge of imperfection,
my doorway into the world of the shunned.

I will try not to hate you.

# II

## Elephants Walking

Curled in a window seat, level with wind-swayed oak,
    aching on a green vinyl pad,
I think of the fortunes spent on the hardwood, wainscot
    study, and the slates fitted
for the arbor walkways, the labor it took to lug bricks out
    to each overly articulated
corner, in which nook a child of fortune, cushion-tassel
    between his fingers, might
look up from his reading to see in the heat waves rising
    over the pale, shimmering
delphinium, a plot miracle perhaps, the strange death
    by spontaneous combustion
in *Our Mutual Friend,* and the child wondering how, why,
    and could it have been?


My childhood bedroom, summer night, one hand marking
    the book, the other's palm
and fingers printing moist, disappearing shadows on the wall.
    Then the college library,
Harkness Hall, and aged, white-cowled Father Benilde
    smelling of coffee, muscatel,
and Old Spice as he opened the doors at 7:30. First in line,
    I was all business, heading
straight to my end of the long, immovable table, to my first
    reading of Dante, a paperback
copy of Ciardi, with its cover of red, grinning, cartoon
    devils, which I had in a fit
of verisimilitude (a word I had just learned)
    charred with a lighter.

My first lines that year: "Butt, butt, base, bale beast.
          I fear your horns not
in the least!" The intended tone was courtly love,
          but the words were
apostrophe to a buffalo in Roger Williams Park,
          one that had leaned
hard into the sagging hurricane fence near my date.
          The lines came to me
as I woke after a nap in the library. I still love
          to sleep in libraries
whenever I can. I fix my head sideways over
          my folded hands,
and make room for the little puddle of drool
          I'll quickly wipe away.
I wake into a barely believable clarity
          throughout my body.
I'm ready to grapple with fate, love, sex,
          the stirrings within.
Over readers and sleepers alike hovers a mist
          or a pollen, and in it
I see words shuttling back and forth like birds.
          In the darkness or dream
something hugely important has been free
          to roam. Grateful,
I say to myself, "Elephants have been walking."


"Son, we must give this country great poetry!"
          decreed the older poet
to my nodding head, as he shook my hand after
          the Crystal Room reading.

Later, as I walked back to my dormitory, sleet
     failing to cool me
I turned his pronoun over and over, thinking
     yes, we do, *we* do.
On the news there was the familiar footage:
     a Phantom run
ending in a hypnotic burst of lit yellow napalm.
     I knew the war
was wrong, but that was why, I claimed, I should go,
     to sing the song
of high lament, to get it into the books. Like Ishmael
     I would sign on
for a three-year voyage under a madman captain.
     Frissons to be had
instantly: a pity-the-youth-soon-dying look in the eyes.
     "Are you crazy?"
asked my girlfriend. But I was filled with vibrant life
     and felt neither suicidal
nor confused when I dialed the Marine recruiter: "Yes,
     I look forward to reporting."
Phone in my lap, I sat sideways, my legs dangling
     over the arms of my red
leather reading chair. A warm spring wind was
     melting the snow
down to bright medallions of ice. I felt clear-headed
     and refreshed.
I just hoped the war would last until I got there.
     Elephants were walking.

# C.O.

*in memoriam: Robert Lowell*

Cold scrambled eggs. Burnt bacon curling
under his slightly cockeyed glasses.
Opera on the stereo, the bay ice-flat
and gray as a naval deck. The shore
rimy and swirling with snow, gusts
rising up to us, a window rattling
behind his "I can breathe out here."

A Sunday in November, 1969,
the morning after Trinity Square
mounted his *Old Glory* trilogy.
Bloody Mary toasts, with celery-stick
swizzles, Worcestershire, horseradish,
and fiery talk about the Narragansetts,
and the colonials who were slavers.

To the sunporch beaming with poets
I carry with me a shadowy prosaic:
orders to Vietnam. A green lieutenant,
shave-headed as a monk, I leave tomorrow
and can't fathom Lowell's question about
the Green Bah-rehs, his breath chopping
the word into hardly intelligible halves.

He takes over and pictures the pajama'd
guerrilla flying out the rear hatch
of the helicopter. He asks me
if I have seen this, and he assumes
I know more than I am saying, me
now the dim, lumpen, and enemy soldier
pleading innocence, ignorance, dismay.

It is as if a vacuum has sucked up
the stray talk, and under his affronted
glare I feel like Hawthorne's young Robin
Molineux bewildered by Boston's
mocking, checker-faced hostility.
I too am blistered by the moment,
and can't believe this is happening.

The china clinks, and talk slowly
resumes while I come to, blinking
like a hammered calf. I hardly know
the abbreviation *C.O.*, but a conscience
must be at work when he leans over
and whispers, "Come back. Intact,"
rhyme nearly full, orders fully meant.

# MALEBOLGE

*Okinawa, 1970*

The Bachelor Officer's Quarters. A Sunday morning,
        my eyes drifting vaguely
over the gypsum ceiling tiles, and over cinder blocks
        as desolate as craters.
Outside the sugar cane hisses, palm fronds clack,
        and a rainstorm darkens
a quadrant of sunlight. Next door, the junior supply
        officer has begun to stir
under his cadre of taped-up Playmates smiling down,
        an air-brushed, backlit
canopy for the boy pasha. In my room, hands behind
        my head, I am deciding
to quit the Marine Corps as a conscientious objector.


*Nei-San* is how it might be spelled phonetically.
        *Sister* or *Miss*
in Japanese, but we use it for the Okinawan maids.
        My roommate has
what is called a "ranch" and spends his weekends
        with our *Nei-San*
in a house outside the gate. How easily we all take
        to the minor pleasures
of empire: *Nei-Sans* to brasso our belt buckles, to wash
        and starch our uniforms,
to spit-polish our boots. Our presence helps, we are told,
        "the local economy."

In the morning when we leave for our work, the *Nei-Sans*
        are setting up, squatting
near the soapy showers, their hot-plates lit, tea-water
        simmering, and Ryukyuan
radio music tuned in. A hard, flattening light pours in
        onto a faded tatami.
I want to linger behind and listen to their jokes about us,
        the young lieutenant-sans.


In Book VI of the *Iliad,* Adrestos falls to Menelaos.
        Wrapping his arms
around the wronged king's knees, Adrestos begs for his life,
        and Menelaos wavers . . .
but as the gods would have it, Agamemnon discovers them
        and rebukes his brother
for softness bordering on the feminine. Then he spears
        Adrestos in the belly,
and as he withdraws the blade, sets his foot on the man's
        ribs for leverage,
saying not even children in the womb are to be spared.
        I dream I am under arms,
helmeted in bronze, with a raised horsehair plume.
        My enemy wrestles me
into submission, and I bite him full on the calf.
        His blood wells up
like a spring, tasting like smoke and quicksilver.
        I sip it and do not die.

The strangest moment in the *Inferno:* when Dante's arms
        are wrapped around
the shoulders of Virgil, who is himself climbing down
        the coarse-haired flank
of Satan, whose enormous body is locked in a lake of ice.
        Suddenly Virgil seems
to be climbing back up, and Dante is bewildered,
        terrified as a child,
and needs to be told they have just passed through
        the core of the fallen
world and they are now hand over hand on their way
        to the earth's other side.


In Tengan, in Camp Smedley T. Butler, named after
        a general who in disgust
at the "banana wars" turned in his medals and quit;
        on a thickly flowered,
half-jungle hillside overlooking the Brig and a sea
        of sugar cane the escapees
loved like life itself; in a white blockhouse, on a spartan
        single bed, in skivvies
and flip-flops, I ask myself again what *would* I
        be willing to trade,
what part of my body, how much of my life would I pay
        for one poem, one true
line about this war. Then a voice not quite my own,
        but close to my face

and as if behind a wire mesh wonders just how grand,
      how filled with epiphany
the poem would have to be if the cost was an arm or more
      belonging to another?


Ganesh, son of Shiva and Parvati, has a pot-bellied
      human torso and an
elephant's head. Beloved by all, he blesses beginnings:
      businesses, marriages,
births. He is also the patron of writers, an inspirer
      of epic poems.
He might as a series of small tremors step through me
      when he rises out
of the cane fields into clouds swollen with rainwater
      from the east.
I wish I could seek his protection in the months it will
      take me to get out.
He would set my penance at twenty years of silence,
      my words curling up
like leaves and blowing away. But even if this were so,
      I would still claim
the quick, half-audible "no" I said out loud was mine.

## TIPPING POINT

Late blue light, the East
    China Sea, a half-mile out . . .
        masked, snorkeled, finned,

rising for air, longing for it,
    and in love with the green
        knife-edged hillsides, the thick

aromatic forests, and not ready
    for the line of B-52's coming in
        low on the horizon, three airplanes

at a time, bomb-empty after
    the all-day run to Vietnam.
        Long, shuddering wings, and predatory,

dorsal tail-fins, underbelly
    in white camouflage, the rest
        jungle-green, saural, as if a gecko had

grown wings, a tail-fin, and
    nightmare proportions. Chest deep,
        on the reef-edge, I think of the war smell

which makes it back here:
    damp red clay, cordite, and fear-salts
        woven into the fabric of everything not

metal: tarps, webbed belts,
    and especially jungle "utes,"
        the utilities, the fatigue blouses

and trousers which were not
    supposed to rip, but breathe,
        and breathe they do—not so much

of death—but rather the long
        living with it, sleeping in it,
                not ever washing your body free of it.

A corporal asked me if he still stank.
        I told him no, and he said,
                "With all due respect, Lieutenant,

I don't believe you." A sea snake,
        *habu*, slips among the corals,
                and I hover while it slowly passes.

My blue surf mat wraps its rope
        around me, tugs inland
                at my hips while I drift over ranges

of thick, branching elkhorn,
        over lilac-pale anemones,
                over the crown-of-thorns starfish,

and urchins spinier than naval
        mines, over mottled slugs,
                half-buried clams, iridescent angelfish.

The commanding general said,
        "Every man has a tipping point,
                a place where his principles give way."

I told him I did not *belong*
        to any nation on earth, but
                a chill shift of wind, its hint of squall

beyond the mountain tells me
        no matter what I said or how,
                it will be a long swim back,
                        complicities in tow.

# III

## STATE LINES

Nevada was nothing but a bubble
of new-blown glass, and I was

at the center, scorching my lungs.
In a rented Sprint, I sped across

the Valley of Fire, scanning the
bleached hardpan, squinting at

The Gorge of the Virgin, a channel
so dry the eyes began to dote on

the clouds gathering up ahead,
on lightning fingering the earth,

on rain unfurling in sheets
that dried out in mid-air.

But in Utah, the land climbed to meet
what it needed, opening its pores

to the rain. I stood on the steaming
Interstate, breathing in juniper and sage,

a smell as sweet and sorrow-laden
as a soul departing.

# Minotaur

*for M.P.B.*

When your madness descended
there was a time when I might
have called it an archangel
announcing the birth of art,

the source of your paintings,
the sardonic, jazzed abstractions,
the washes you said were portraits
of Lords and Ladies, but in which

there were only color and pain.
Tally sheets of the spirit,
toteboards with odds-on listings
of what was left of the divine,

we said. Maybe so. I do know
there are plainer ways of being
lost, and plainer meanings:
the significances in wire mesh,

the "left after you step off
the elevator, then left again,"
red tape on the floor to follow
past the boiling kitchen smells,

the starch-heavy air of laundry,
and then left again, to a buzzer,
a lock that works off a card.
"Look," says the nurse opening

your door. He reassures us
the sheets and floors are clean.
In the next room, someone is
saying, *I* know, *I* know.

I feel like one of those youths
brought in tribute from the great
state of reason, the Athenian world
of my sunlight and striving.

Touching your hand, I think
of the cruelty in that myth
of the sovereign, half-human
devouring beast. I pity now

his parched and swollen tongue,
his jaw moving unwilled,
and I fear the mania
driving him to toss his head.

## SUNDAY, AFTER A STORM

We listen, and the reef crackles
with its self-making. We read
that when the great humpbacks
are mating the harmonics of their
cries pass right through the bodies
of divers, stirring in them joy.

On the shore, a land crab flares out
its arms at the colossi peering down.
When it flees, it tumbles over itself,
and comes up staring back at us.
The sea grape's limbs scrape at each
other, squeak like children dreaming.
Cicadas rouse to their first call
to arms for the day. The great flag
of the palm tree rustles and sighs.

We listen, and our own words rise,
or seem to, from what we have heard.

## STILLNESS IN SOUTH CAROLINA

It was older than the red barns,
older than the frog pond for the cattle,
than the road up Clark Hill, and the live oak
colonnade leading to the rich man's brasses.

Older too than the ox-blood and the idea
of honor, or the dream of dominance.
It was a stillness of light pouring in,
of cooling airs that made nothing move.

The stillness of tamarack pumping sap,
of the deer mid-stream baling its ears.
The history that could not be changed,
and locusts crying out everywhere.

## DEMBY IN THE RIVER

*. . . if he did not come out at the third call,*
*[Mr. Gore] would shoot him.*

Frederick Douglass, *Narrative*

If I were the eight-year-old witness,
I might have imagined minnows swimming
out to rescue, to touch the man's ankles
in the cloud-swirl, to nibble on what
his feet had churned up. I might have
heard the reeds whispering yes into
the green, oily waters, telling him
to be as still as he wanted, and to stay.

If I were the eight-year-old witness,
I might have imagined the flare,
and the report sounding like a hammer,
and the echo hammering out over the bend
in the Tuckahoe. I might have imagined
that the desert began here, that nothing
living could ever enter, or bathe, or drink
here again. I might have said to no one
but myself that the creek lapping seemed
to say *Egypt, Egypt, Egypt,* again and again.

## ROGER WILLIAMS, HIS *KEY INTO THE LANGUAGE OF AMERICA*

He stood at the heart of a grayness of soul
    he sometimes approximated
        by speaking of fogs and miasma.

He thought himself a New Man climbing over
    the oarlocks, stepping out onto the point
        jutting into the sea-plumed bay.

Soon he would gather the immense, bearded
    clusters of mussels and drop them
        clattering into an oaken bucket.

In that they hung awash and clung to the rocks,
    they were like words the Lord
        had seeded the fallen world with.

And since creation was to be of use, he would pry
    open what he found here, knowing
        the many would resolve into One.

Yet, in the very sinews of the tongue he could feel
    the struggle re-enacted: them wary
        on the rock-strewn shore, and him,

scraping the rudder through the shallows, declaring
    "What Cheer, Ne-top?" the English
        hard on the native word for brother.

## MAYAN FIGURES IN STONE

O we could be solemn and teach
you, or pretend
to teach you some lessons still

in what it means to worship and
be worshipped.
We could show you the sense

of heaving the body upward,
the purpose of
climbing in pursuit of the spirit.

We could show you holds in the living
rock, reveal
the corbel arches embedded in

the secret center, the ceremonially
intended replica
of all the balanced forces locked

together in silicates of belief.
We could sweat
you through one human step after

another, parting the layers of heat,
pressing you
to us, letting you hear the thin, wet

chatter of limestone, the whispers
of quartz with
granite, the stone telling the truth

about sacrifice, how we delivered
ourselves freely,
releasing our hopes like birds

we had taught never to return,
how we too
hovered, not ever wanting to die.

## LAZARUS

Before the intervention
the exhalation had begun.
The spirit hid within the ear,
and what he felt, therefore,
became what he thought he heard.

The place where they placed him
pressed in upon the drum
and sounded like a sandy bank,
a gravelly run of waterway
with weeds whispering in a bend.

A mill wheel slotted in between
a cedar stump and the open mouth
was, as was ordered, heaved aside,
but it was not his shouted name
within the cave that made him rise.

What he heard was the scraping
of a hoe, and the locusts' whine.
What he felt was the liquid,
half-hesitant thing come rushing in,
and light, like human eyes.

## HERONS

In a gray curve of tidal flat,
scores of herons stock still,

heads cocked at oblique angles,
water ruffling at their legs.

The herring see only sets of yellow
weed-stems rising bolt upright.

They cannot imagine the orange,
unlidded eye of God, how poised

it is, how steady its aim.

# IV

## WARTIME

*The soul is always beautiful,*
*The universe is in order, everything is in its place.*

Whitman, *The Sleepers*

i.

Oranges, clementines, green daffodil stems, yellow
horns, good light. Our mahogany table.
    I wonder how many loaded bombers
      flew from Maine.
    I wonder what the ground trembling
      felt like within it.

Here in Belmont, the paperboy rings our bell
saying he's got the flu,
      and could we call his Dad to take
      him home. It is wet,
    January, but Dad does not thank me.
      He is disappointed in Mikey.

One line that stays from the *Agamemnon* is about
the storm that brought
      the Argives home from Troy:
        "the sea bloomed with corpses."
      The way wildflowers in the
        desert overnight spring.

ii.

The première. Snow
      in oversized flakes.
        Predictions way too low.

In the room of negotiation
      ministers defter than ghosts
        touch for the cameras.

We joke, the student and I:
>he needs a design, a logo
>>for the cover of his magazine.

I suggest *Death Before*
>*Dishonor*, in scrolled letters,
>>heraldic, under crossed daggers,

or maybe it's only one,
>the memory is dim: blue
>>and green lines of bright tattoo,

with red ink inserted
>under the skin and shaped
>>to look like perfect drops.

"That's the one you want, right?"

iii.

Years ago in the deserts of Utah
>I would go days without words,

drugged with red rock, hiking in the Maze,
>relieved of my life, touching the rock wall,

a chipped Kokopelli flute, fingertips
>tracing the curved arch, the brittle spine.

Now this: printed on grainy manila,
>page three, an earnest, moonfaced G.I.

at the window of a burned-out truck,
a corpse fried to the seat springs. Caption:

*Iraqi Dead* . . . No shit.
The G.I.'s lips teeter on the edge of hilarity.

Thinks he's really seeing something.
How solemn the shape, stretched and still.

Two of us: pausing, gazing, bending, stopping.

iv.

Like the commanders from their maps
I leave the television and take to bed
the play-symbol derricks, tanks, planes,
the corridors of regimentally shaded terrain.

Out of the white nub of the earphone
I siphon in the talk radio. *Traitor,*
a woman flings the word as if
it could flare in our common night.

When I wake, the *Quick boys!*
of Owen's nightmare
circles over the low, undisturbed
places where the poison has settled.

In the morning paper's quippy
column I catch a whiff:
"As for the old conscientious objection . . .
better leave it off the resumé."

v.

On the television, the fishbone-lean little general who is fond of the metaphor, "the fog of war." No one, he says, can see the whole picture. No one knows what the other fellow is doing. Sometimes, he says, it's not even clear to yourself what you are doing.

I remember my first morning in the Marine Corps. Long before sunlight, we were outside standing at attention, eyes locked straight ahead, feet at a forty-five degree angle, heels touching, and soles on the painted footprints which told the platoon how to form itself. The drill instructor announced that on his command each of us would turn right and step off with the left foot, and that thereafter the left foot would always be striking the deck to the sound of *Laeouff*. The right foot, he said, would be landing to the sound of *Heidle*. Strung together, they composed a marching cadence which sounded like this:

*Laeouff—heidle—laeouw—heidle—laeouw—heidle—louw*
*. . . laeouff—heidle—louw*
*. . . laeouff—heidle—louw*

Cadence, in other words, began with four beats, followed by a pair of trimeter lines. Yet every drill instructor put a signature on his cadence by cutting and twirling syllables like a scat singer. Along with the feel of improvisation, there was a thread of the joyful, as if the instructor were an outsized woodthrush presiding over a scale that nature had allotted and commanded him to sing. It was a beautiful sound floating over our heads and governing, guiding us to the mess hall in the early morning darkness.

Had I been asked that morning I would have said I understood *Billy Budd*. I would have said it was a parable about how the world cannot tolerate the persistently innocent. I would have said it was the archetypal "inside narrative," about wars in the soul, not wars of the European imperium. In pidgen, "Christ and Billy, same-same."

Today, though, I think of the strangest moment in that story. Just before Vere signals the hangman, Billy shouts without a trace of the fatal stammer, "God bless Captain Vere." Despite being appalled at what is happening to Billy, the crew repeats his blessing in antiphonal response. Maybe they are being ironic. Maybe they so love the Handsome Sailor they will repeat whatever he says. As Billy's body rises in the fleece-lined dawn, the warship beneath them cuts through moderate seas, a nation unto itself, ponderously cannoned.

vi.

A woman on the radio describing her mother's wounds:
World War II, the Philippines, an airport strafing
left her with six scooped-out, star-shaped scars
on her back and thighs, each with a rough ridge
of flesh the child who then believed in the sweet,
oily powers of Jergens hoped she could make vanish
if only she worked the lotion in deeply enough.

> *These were wonders we had no*
> *account whereof. Thus we questioned*
> *the child vigorously . . .*

How many times, she was asked, did you try this?

> *and in time*
> *she admitted slipping through keyholes,*
> *and had upon occasion been a cat,*
> *a mare, a stoat.*

War, she answered, disfigures everyone.

> *All matter is dead. We know this.*

vii.

What is it then between us?

Is it a cold snap, the Square empty, a taxi breaking
from line and heading straight at me,
its wake whipping into chill benzene wind?

Is it the newsstand in silver light, tall glossies
declaring the war in thick, opulent letters,
announcing we are stoic and firm?

There is something in us that loves this.

It lances a pressure, leeches a poison,
shades the trivial in lurid color: O sweet
portents, O death which helps us feel!

This is how our uneasiness works,
all our goods waving like the legumes
of the prairie under an utterly empty blue.

Imagine the pearly chenille on the bed,
the Smith & Wesson revolver oiled,
the polished holster glinting with prohibition,

the miraculous blue tint of the forging,
the sweet heft, the woodpanel grip,
almost human to the touch, notched.

Or think of your own foot hard on the accelerator,
eight lanes from Logan down to two in the tunnel,
and the fenders nosing near, *Fuck you!*

Or the subway roaring under the city on the hill,
the gold dome of the State House rising
like a mortar shell from its tube.

Step off the train and ride the escalator up,
into the cold snap, the Square,
the taxi heading straight for you.

Sometimes I think there's nothing left between us.
Not even words.

viii.

*What was the state of your knowledge concerning*
*eternal life last spring?*

I knew the spirits of the dead were around.
I believed, but did not know for certain,
that they inhabited the forms of the beautiful.

*Please be more specific.*

In certain slants of light, in sea-feathers
on a jetty, in the rustling of palms.
Perhaps there were others less congenial.

*Did you recognize any?*

Of course not. They were anonymous,
abstract. More like rhythms.
I gave them names of those I loved.

*Go on.*

I remember they were plentiful that year,
a swarming light and shadow play,
abundant, yet easy to ignore.

V

## LINES AFTER BUSON

We were—there were many of us then—
talking about leaving. You mentioned
his haiku: "You leave, I stay,
two autumns," and I felt the chill

of the ice skimmed off the birdbath,
and its beauty, as if we had held it up
as lens. You said leaving should
make us more alert to loss and that

being was in some way attention.
The color of it bleeds now into sunlight
and onto every leaf. I bend for
a bright one. Even the ice disappears.

# RESCUE

I wake and listen to a machine
growl through last night's snow,
and I remember trains coupling
in the railyard by the cemetery.

I remember being frightened,
calling out, my mother coming
to calm me and explain why
the work went on all night.

I also remember their sounds,
those I didn't dare ask about.
I would curl and recoil,
wall them out with my pillow.

Now the sound of whatever love
they had comes to me like a letter
I tear open with a pleasure
I never dreamed I would have.

I want to run into their room,
climb in under the covering years,
breathe in their strong night smell,
and tell them both they will not die.

## HOSPITAL FOOD

After they bring the usual fare,
the canned wedges of peach,
the raspberry jello, the bland
concoctions of gravied meats,
the milk in waxy little cartons,
after all that for which I have
no stomach, my husband will arrive
with my robe and nightgown,
my rosary beads blessed by the Pope,
and my purse with the hidden check.
He will arrive under a cloud of
nervous energy, breath whiskied
and ripe, and as he unpacks the bag,
he will be saying, "Just a minute,
just a *minute!*" And I will feel again
his wish that I were already gone,
and his eyes when I meet them
will be as hateful to me as his words
about the need for a wheelchair,
or the danger of the rugs, and how
I cannot tie my own shoes. He will
say then he cannot understand
why I am crying, and I will tell him,
"I am not. I *am not!*"

## WALDEN

Water silver-green as the pickerel
which trail my shadow underneath.

Mulch, scrap limbs, snowmelt springs,
and nothing too large or deep.

Drift, flat on your back, a mote.
"One, two, three," says a mother to her boy

when she heaves him up by his foot,
and "Keep your mouth shut."

In Lourdes the pilgrims line up
to jettison their pale, sweatworn devices.

To our school the nuns would bring back
blue bottles of that "water of life."

Here a pregnant woman enters the pond,
right hand stirring before her belly.

The pond as best it can makes way.

# CERTAIN OBLIQUITIES, AND THEN LOSS

The nurse said I should come down
immediately, that I could go
either to "the IC unit,
or the family home."

*

My father waited in the bright
and empty little room. He stood
when he saw me, and held his arms
out wide as if he'd been caught
drinking and driving,
had caused an accident,
and I would blame him.

*

It was 6 p.m. when the phone first
rang. All the way down 128 the sun
had done its part, the light sifting
even into the lobby, gilding the wax
and the sills of her west-facing room,
making the leaves on the copper
tree my brother had given her
shimmer when I entered.

*

I am sitting now in a garden,
having raked the leaves,
pulled out and stored away
the tomato stakes. The hose
is coiled. I threw out the last
of the basil. The storm windows
are already down, and I couldn't
hear the phone ring if you paid me.

*

She was gone before I got there.

## BRISTLECONE

Sometimes a tree will be there
when you need it most, when
you realize that you've been
breathing too long in the high,

thinned out air. Maybe you've
staggered, tripped on a rock
you warned yourself about,
but tripped on anyway. Marmots

may be signaling your coming,
and you could answer with your
own set of clicks and whistles,
but all this would only deepen

the dizziness, the spin of nausea,
the dread combining with delight
at reaching the rim of the canyon.
Below, the rock shapes waver,

and you are not the first to think
they look like the dead. You want
to run after them, to tug and plead.
The feeling as it rises has its own

strong winds. You know that
lightning and rain will be coming.
You stand in one of the eroded
places seeking out that tree.

## STARLIGHT MINTS

i.
For months I have spoken on behalf of my aged
        and inarticulate father.
I try to be orderly describing his symptoms:

inner to outer, morning to night. Prostate cancer.
        Emphysema. Both
advanced. In the former, the home of maleness,

the fountain of youth, the spring of come,
        the walnut, however
you want it, has, in my father's own words,

"turned bad." In the other disease, the far reaches
        of his lungs have begun
to explode, tissue pulling itself apart, searching for

any pink remnant still capable of the oxygen
        exchange. Hunched
in the wheelchair beside me, the man is drowning.

ii.
I, 45, in perfect health, too fat for my own good,
        but filled with a sense
of lasting, the world of the body still mine, while his

world belongs to his memory and needs too much air
        for him to bother even
to recall. The contrast-gainer, I cannot help but dote

on the present tense of the bodies of passing nurses,
    their nylons whispering.
Discreet, attentive as a twelve-year-old to the shapes

under the underwear, to thin fabric, to bra-straps,
    to lips and nails brightened
by Eros, not the mighty, vehement god, but a daimon,

flickering in white light among the newly washed
    and the mostly well,
making me ache for the *little death,* its salt smell of youth.

iii.
Two years ago I peeked at his chart. The nurse said
    his body was "wasted."
He has lost a pound a month ever since. Eighty-five

is what he tips. His biceps are as thin as my wrists.
    His jade ring now spins
around the bone of his middle finger. His ribs tube

like a birdcage. When he walks he looks drunken,
    as if the planet wobbled
on its axis underneath him. He fidgets with a *People,*

then unwraps a Starlight Mint. The sound his mouth
    makes is not exactly
a smacking of his lips, but more a devoted sucking

that I can't stand to listen to. He is after little puffs
    of air over the candy.
"Try not to be so loud," I whisper, feeling better

68

that I have made my real wishes known to him,
       but then he forgets and I,
ill-tempered and embarrassed, need to tell him again.

iv.
What has passed between us in the forms of language
       has been plainer than
doorknobs. He is either "pretty good," or "not bad,"

or "no good," each of which might denote the identical
       condition. If he were God,
ours might be a world where language didn't matter.

Words for him were at best an affliction, bees
       suddenly infesting
the rotten eaves of a clapboard house. As a boy,

he stuttered, and I can only imagine the wrenching
       self-discipline it took him,
as he said, to straighten out. He used to shout at me,

"6-B! 6-B!" this, his coded complaint that at ten,
       with his father dead,
his mother had made him go to work pumping gas,

changing tires. The station a school where
       he learned the language
of practical men: fillerup, fin, *fucking engine!*

v.
Poet? Poetry? Could he have predicted a son like me?
        Once when I accused him
of not wanting to know what my life was really like,

he summoned a breath to say, "You'll never know
        how much." A sentence
with a sentence-sound, as Frost would have noted,

you had to reckon with, which is what I am doing
        when they call for us.
I wheel him in and help him stand. The nurse asks

how is he feeling. He steadies himself at the edge
        of the papered table,
his Jockeys down, baggy on his thighs. "Oooh Walter . . .

there's practically nothing left of you."

Nearly transparent flesh, pelvic blades, and pressed
        to his hip, the cellophane
wrap from a Starlight Mint. Not one of us says a word.

## LOOSE ENDS

I met my father at the empty ski lift
    shortly after supper.

This was unexpected, even for a dream.
    It was summer,

and he loved the fact he was breathing
    normally again.

His weight was back too, and I made
    a caliper with thumb

and forefinger to measure his bicep
    and said, "not bad,

pretty good," the way he used to.
    He seemed to revel

in the bright thin air, and set a quick
    pace up. He had

his legs and did not stagger or work
    between handholds

which brought us to the tree line where
    we sat under a pine

whose trunk was a cool, emerald moss.
    We drank a mint tea

neither of us had carried or brewed,
    and thus began our talk

with a sense of abundance and thanks.
    We bartered versions

of the past. He said he understood my
    anger and admitted

his failures in the world had turned him
    vicious sometimes,

but he wanted me to acknowledge how
    much he had lost,

our house on Camp Street, the station,
    even his car.

We went on like this until the light
    dwindled to a gray

glow behind the massif wall. A wind
    had begun to shake

the low, leathery scrub, and I felt a twinge
    of the urgent as he

pulled himself up. "Let's leave it now at that,"
    he said in a tone so full

of conviction I didn't want to argue with him.
    I had his arm in my hand

as we walked toward some lupine and a yellow
    flower whose name

I did not know and thought for a second he might,
    but when I awoke

I was back under the knotty pine, watching
    mist rising from a meadow

and feeling more than a little guilt, as if
    I had turned him in,

helped him over, or let him go.

## RED'S MEADOW

*for  W.L.M.*

In the night, endless switchbacks, with pine
and fir leaning over smooth blacktop
and growing out of pale, pumice topsoil.
Morning: horse smell through the window,
sugar pines, scattered cones, larkspur, a stream.

When I called you, I shouted into the pay phone:
"A beautiful place, the middle of the mountains!"
I don't know what I expected you to say.
Later I heard you had cursed the nurse
for a pint she found hidden under a cushion.

Right before you died I too said no whiskey,
not on an empty stomach, yet I poured you
a shot anyway. You barely sipped it, but the smell
must have been like an old friend, a comfort.
Then you said, "I'm near the end."

I flinched and smiled and loved the way
the words thickened the minute, resisting
what hurried along. I should have pushed
back too when the intern used the word
"pretzel" as a verb to describe you folding

your legs up and in. I should have said,
even here among the machines mapping
the heart's long climb, its leap from range
to range, even here in these night mountains
is a meadow, a *lea,* a *place of light shining.*

## THE AFTERLIFE ON SQUAW PEAK

No matter the machines
with their silent flywheels
and strange swinging on cables
that helped you get here.
No matter the masts of measurement
and reason which the earnest
have strapped to the summit.
There is still the terrible loneliness
of the next valley over
to convince you with its quartz
and granite flashing like ice
and its meadow emptied of the human.
Flower blossoms—little trumpets
of delight—shudder at your feet.
The shale you stand on is splattered
with bright lichens. You join them
by laying low out of the wind
to look up the flower's name–
*scarlet penstemon*—and you have
that small, but significant human
pleasure of finally knowing.
This high, you have trouble breathing,
and feeling sleepy, you find

a place without thorns. Your eyelids
tighten, and the wind carries voices
that seem shaken, as if assembled
at your sickbed.

                       When you wake,
you note how little seems changed.
You perhaps wonder where you came from
and why. You want to take off
your clothes and mark where you have
lain. Now the wind sounds out clearly
and says this is the mountain
of forgiveness, and that the work
will be to traverse the empty spaces
with meaning. If those you love
glimpse you, it will be in the form
of a red-tail fox crossing at dusk
into the wood stand, and because they
have loved you, they will watch
as long as you let them. They will not
harm you, so swears the wind,
not this close to heaven.

Susan Unterberg

## About the Author

Fred Marchant was born in Providence, Rhode
Island. He is a graduate of Brown University and the
University of Chicago. He has taught at Harvard
University and Boston University, and is currently
Chair of the Humanities and Modern Languages
Department at Suffolk University in Boston. From
1968 to 1970 he was a lieutenant in the Marine Corps,
and was one of the first officers ever to be discharged
honorably as a conscientious objector. His poetry and
reviews have appeared in such journals as *AGNI,
Ploughshares, Harvard Review, Gettysburg Review,* and
*Poetry Northwest.* He has been awarded fellowships from
MacDowell, Yaddo, and the Ucross Foundation.
*Tipping Point* is his first full-length collection.

## About the Artist

Nona Hershey's work has been shown internation-
ally, and can be seen in numerous public collections,
including those of the Metropolitan Museum of Art,
the Library of Congress, Calcographia Nazionale
(Rome), Crakow National Museum, and Yale Univer-
sity Art Gallery. Director of the printmaking program
at Tyler School of Art in Rome until 1990, she cur-
rently teaches printmaking at the Massachusetts
College of Art in Boston.

*Tipping Point* is the winner of the 1993 Word Works Washington Prize. Fred Marchant's manuscript was selected from 344 manuscripts that were submitted by American poets.

FIRST READERS:
Jamie Brown
Joetta Harty
Sally Murray James
Michael Schaffner
Ian Walton
Leslie Wilson
Ron Wilson


SECOND READERS:
Catherine Harnett-Shaw
Anne Sheldon


FINAL JUDGES:
Karren L. Alenier
J.H. Beall
Howard Gofreed, *Project Co-Director*
Barbara Goldberg
Jim Henley, *Project Co-Director*
Robert Sargent

Other Books in the WORD WORKS Series:

| | |
|---|---|
| Alenier, Karren L. | *Wandering on the Outside* |
| Beall, J.H. | *Hickey, the Days . . .* |
| * Bradley, John | *Love-In-Idleness: The Poetry of Roberto Zingarello* |
| * Bursk, Christopher | *The Way Water Rubs Stone* |
| Cavalieri, Grace | *Creature Comforts* |
| * Goldberg, Barbara | *Berta Broadfoot and Pepin the Short: A Merovingian Romance* |
| **McEuen, James | *Snake Country* |
| * Magarrell, Elaine | *Blameless Lives* |
| * Moore, Barbara | *Farewell to the Body* |
| Sargent, Robert | *Aspects of a Southern Story* |
| Sargent, Robert | *Woman From Memphis* |
| * Shomer, Enid | *Stalking the Florida Panther* |
| **Tham, Hilary | *Bad Names for Women* |
| * White, Nancy | *Sun, Moon, Salt* |

  * *Washington Prize Winners*
** *Capital Collection*

WORD WORKS Anthologies:

| | |
|---|---|
| Alenier, Karren L. | *Whose Woods These Are* |
| Bursk, Christopher | *Cool Fire* (A chapbook from the Community for Creative Non-Violence workshop) |
| Dor, Moshe | *The Stones Remember: Native Israeli Poetry\** |
| Goldberg, Barbara | |
| Leshem, Giora | |
| Parry, Betty | *The Unicorn and the Garden* |

  * *Witter Bynner Foundation Award*

## About WORD WORKS

The Word Works, a nonprofit literary organization, publishes contemporary poetry in collector's editions. Since 1981, the organization has sponsored the Washington Prize, an award of $1,000 to a living American poet. Each summer, Word Works presents free poetry programs at the Joaquin Miller Cabin in Washington, DC's Rock Creek Park. Annually, two high school students debut at the Miller Cabin Series as winners of the Young Poets Competition.

Since Word Works was founded in 1974, programs have included: "In the Shadow of the Capitol," a symposium and archival project on the African-American intellectual community in segregated Washington, DC; the Gunston Arts Center Poetry Series (including Ai, Carolyn Forché, Stanley Kunitz, Linda Pastan, among others); the Poet-Editor panel discussions at the Bethesda Writer's Center (including John Hollander, Maurice English, Anthony Hecht, Josephine Jacobsen, among others); Poet's Jam, a multi-arts program series featuring poetry in performance; and many other events and educational programs such as a poetry workshop at the Center for Creative Non-Violence (CCNV) shelter.

Past grants have been awarded by the National Endowment for the Arts, the National Endowment for the Humanities, the DC Commission the Arts and Humanities, the Witter Bynner Foundation, and others, including many generous private patrons.

Word Works is a member of the Poetry Committee of the Greater Washington, DC Area, which is centered at the Folger Shakespeare Library. The WORD WORKS has established an archive of artistic and administrative materials in the Washington Writing Archive housed in the George Washington University Gelman Library.

Please enclose a self-addressed, stamped envelope with all inquiries.